# The Future of the Human Race;
## or a great, glorious, and peaceful revolution, near at hand, to be effected through the agency of departed spirits of good and superior men and women.

Robert Owen

*The Future of the Human Race; or a great, glorious, and peaceful revolution, near at hand, to be effected through the agency of departed spirits of good and superior men and women.*
Owen, Robert
British Library, Historical Print Editions
British Library
1853
8°.
10006.df.25.

## The BiblioLife Network

This project was made possible in part by the BiblioLife Network (BLN), a project aimed at addressing some of the huge challenges facing book preservationists around the world. The BLN includes libraries, library networks, archives, subject matter experts, online communities and library service providers. We believe every book ever published should be available as a high-quality print reproduction; printed on- demand anywhere in the world. This insures the ongoing accessibility of the content and helps generate sustainable revenue for the libraries and organizations that work to preserve these important materials.

The following book is in the "public domain" and represents an authentic reproduction of the text as printed by the original publisher. While we have attempted to accurately maintain the integrity of the original work, there are sometimes problems with the original book or micro-film from which the books were digitized. This can result in minor errors in reproduction. Possible imperfections include missing and blurred pages, poor pictures, markings and other reproduction issues beyond our control. Because this work is culturally important, we have made it available as part of our commitment to protecting, preserving, and promoting the world's literature.

## GUIDE TO FOLD-OUTS, MAPS and OVERSIZED IMAGES

In an online database, page images do not need to conform to the size restrictions found in a printed book. When converting these images back into a printed bound book, the page sizes are standardized in ways that maintain the detail of the original. For large images, such as fold-out maps, the original page image is split into two or more pages.

Guidelines used to determine the split of oversize pages:

- Some images are split vertically; large images require vertical and horizontal splits.
- For horizontal splits, the content is split left to right.
- For vertical splits, the content is split from top to bottom.
- For both vertical and horizontal splits, the image is processed from top left to bottom right.

# THE FUTURE

OF

# THE HUMAN RACE;

OR A

GREAT, GLORIOUS, AND PEACEFUL REVOLUTION,
NEAR AT HAND,

TO BE EFFECTED

THROUGH THE AGENCY OF DEPARTED SPIRITS

OF

GOOD AND SUPERIOR MEN AND WOMEN.

BY

ROBERT OWEN.

LONDON:
PUBLISHED BY EFFINGHAM WILSON, ROYAL EXCHANGE;
J. CLAYTON AND SON, 223, PICCADILLY; AND
SOLD BY ALL BOOKSELLERS.

1853.

*Truth alone can make man good, wise, and happy.*

*The first coming of this Truth was through Jesus Christ, an inspired medium from his birth, to teach the world the necessity for it to acquire* universal love *and* charity.

*The second coming of Truth is* now, *to teach the world* how to acquire and practise *universal love and charity, and thus, not in words but in action, to prove their love to God.*

ROBERT OWEN.

# DEDICATED

TO THOSE WHO ABOVE ALL THINGS DESIRE TO ATTAIN

A KNOWLEDGE OF TRUTH;

WHO HAVE MORAL COURAGE TO FOLLOW WHEREVER IT LEADS;

WHOSE MINDS EXPAND BEYOND THE PREJUDICES OF CLASS,

CREED, COUNTRY, AND COLOUR;

WHO LOVE HUMANITY;

WHOSE ACTIVE ENDEAVOURS ARE TO DO GOOD TO ALL,

AND

TO SECURE THE PERMANENT HAPPINESS OF OUR RACE.

# THE FUTURE
## OF THE
# HUMAN RACE.

It is not the philosophy of words which is now required; but it is the actual practice that will make the human race good, wise, and happy.

For the human race to become good, wise, and happy, it must be surrounded from birth with those conditions only which can produce this result.

This result can be attained to its full and desirable extent, only when all of human kind can be surrounded with those conditions which shall train and educate every one from and before birth — physically, intellectually, morally, and practically—to the full extent of the powers of the germ or spirit of each individual; and this is the only mode by which all individuals, including the entire of the human race, can attain the greatest amount of permanent advantages. These conditions may be now commenced in Europe, America, Asia, and Africa, at once; and, with the new physical powers now acquired by society, may be made rapidly to extend over the world, and peaceably to supersede the existing most injurious conditions which prevail throughout the entire of society over our globe, and through which, sovereigns are among the greatest sufferers.

The first impression upon all people, as all have so far been trained and educated, will be, that to create such conditions is impossible, and to place the rulers and wealthy in better positions impracticable. But, instead of being impossible, they will be found, upon trial, after a short experience, to be not only possible, but most easy of practice.

It will be found that it will be far less difficult to introduce and maintain this change of conditions and mode of governing the human race, than to continue the present practices of the population of the world as they exist to-day in all countries.

To continue the present system by which society is governed in all states and among all people, is now become impracticable. The aggregate of knowledge now acquired is too great to admit the continuance of a system of thinking and acting so erroneous and weak, and so directly opposed to the well-being, well-doing, and happiness of every one over the earth, without a single exception. There is not one of our race who is not a grievous sufferer by the continuance of this system—a system now discovered to be false in principle and most injurious in all its practice.

Even the high and mighty of the earth, as they are called and considered by the deluded mass, are physical and mental slaves to this system of falsehood and evil, and do not, through their lives, possess the state of mind and feeling which alone deserves the name of happiness; for in their position they cannot be educated and placed to become good and wise.

The language of truth is unknown to these parties to a greater extent than to all below them in station. Yet until principles shall be introduced to make the language of truth universal, goodness, wisdom, and happiness, must remain unknown. Falsehood is directly opposed to goodness, wisdom, and happiness—yet the language of the world at this day is the language of falsehood. It is so from necessity; because the principle on which society has been based is false; and with that principle for its foundation, the language of truth becomes impracticable; and with the language of falsehood, the creation and maintenance of good conditions are impossible.

The question now to be put for the calm and deliberate consideration of the human mind is—

"Will it be better, in future, to continue the language of falsehood, the necessary crimes which it creates against human nature, with the unavoidable miseries thence arising,—or is it more desirable to have the language of truth, with its necessary consequences—goodness, wisdom, and happiness, now introduced to all people?

Mankind can have only the one or the other of these states. The former only has been experienced from the creation of man to this period; but many now begin to feel that there is *something wrong at the foundation of society.*

The all important question to the present generation is, to ascertain *whether human nature is now sufficiently developed to admit at once the language of truth and the creation of good conditions only, by changing one palpable falsehood for one palpable truth.*

With the belief taught to all from their birth, that each one forms his own physical, intellectual, moral, and practical character, (or forms himself,) and is responsible for what he is formed to be, to think, and to act, the language of truth is impracticable. And until the universal and undeviating language of truth shall be practicable, goodness, wisdom, and happiness, will be unknown, and impracticable of attainment.

Neither, while society shall be based on this

principle of falsehood, can there be unity of feeling, interest, and action, among the human race, or charity, peace, and goodwill among mankind. With this principle of society, it must continue, as heretofore, irrational in principle, and corrupt—nay, insane in practice.

It is now to be ascertained whether the population of the world is sufficiently developed to acquire the requisite moral courage now to abandon at once the principle which creates the necesity for the language of falsehood, and openly to adopt the principle which alone can make the language of truth possible and practicable. It is now known, and is worthy of everlasting remembrance, that until the mind of man shall become dead to the principle of falsehood and alive to the principle of truth, it cannot be born again. It is the principle of falsehood which keeps man in bondage to ignorance, sin, and misery. It is the principle of truth which can alone regenerate man, and make him a rational, consistent, reasonable, and happy being.

It has been stated in the fourth number of my Review, that the language of truth is incompatible, nay impracticable, with any of the religions of the world, with law-made unnatural marriages, or with private property. As soon as society shall be composed of good conditions only,—that is, of the best conditions which men can now create in conformity with human nature, and when men shall be trained and educated within these natural, good, and superior conditions, there will not be the slightest use in any one of these religions, in any unnatural law-made marriages, or in private property. But as long as any one of these shall remain, it will be an insurmountable obstacle to the attainment of unity, charity, and love, to the language of truth, and to the peace and happiness of the human race.

The only rational or useful religion is, to increase the happiness of God's creation. Man can do no other good to God; and it is now evident that he has been created by the Creating Power of the Universe to accomplish this result. This Power, hitherto and yet incomprehensible to the human faculties, is too good, wise, great, and independent of his creation, to derive gratification from human flattery, or from being told by man what he previously knows far better than man can tell him. A superior being could not be gratified by the flattery or worship of that which he had created—it would be self-flattery and self-worship, and inconsistent with infinite wisdom and power.

To all appearance the Great Creating Power of the universe is progressing man and the universe to attain in due time their full extent of happiness.

And man will be in possession of this state of his existence, when he shall have acquired the knowledge and moral courage to surround his offspring with the conditions which are alone in accordance with the nature which has been given to him; and it is through these conditions alone, that the language of truth can be introduced among men, and be made to become the language of the human race.

When law-made marriages shall be abandoned, and men and women shall have become rational, through the good and superior conditions in accordance with their nature by which they are to be surrounded, and when the language of truth shall take the place of the present universal language of falsehood, then will they know each other's feelings and thoughts, even as they know their own, and their union and conduct, unrestricted by man's irrational laws, will be natural and pure, and will in a high degree promote their permanent happiness, the happiness of their children, and the happiness of the human race, and jealousy, or counteractions of the feelings between men and women, will be unknown.

It is only under this natural state of humanity that the children of the human race can be made to become rational and superior beings, physically, intellectually, morally, and practically. It is only under these arrangements that children can be relieved from the evil effects of false and unnatural parental associations, from the evils of family training and education, and from being made family-selfish, and unjust to all other families. It is only thus that a true equality, according to age and personal qualities, can be attained. It is only thus that men and women can be trained and educated from birth to become truly good, wise, and happy, and that the human race can become superior citizens of the world, and be united to form one cordial brotherhood. It is thus only that man can be so trained and placed that he will love his neighbour as himself, and have no enemies to forgive. It is thus only that charity and love can be made to become universal in practice, and that peace and goodwill can be made to be permanent over the earth.

As soon as society shall know how to create good conditions, and when these shall have been created, private property will naturally and gradually cease to exist. For private property and truth, charity, love, justice, goodness, wisdom, unity, and happiness, can never co-exist. The practice of private property is possible only in a state of low development of the human faculties, and while they are passing from this condition to a rational state of existence,—to a higher development of the superior faculties of our race.

The object aimed at by private property is to give to the individuals possessing more of it than others, privileges not to be attained by their less wealthy neighbours; and to give them power to oppress those who are less wealthy,

It is supposed that the system of private property enables society to create more wealth in the aggregate than would be obtained by a properly constituted system of public property. Yet no supposition could be more erroneous. Private property is one of the greatest bars to the creation of wealth, as well as one of the greatest immediate causes of crime and of repulsive feeling among the human race. It stands in the way of all great, noble, and beneficial arrangements for the general benefit of society.

It is imagined also that the possessor of private property enjoys advantages which he could not obtain under a system of public property. But when this subject shall be fairly opened to the public mind, and shall be understood in all its bearings, it will be discovered that under the rational arrangements of public property each one in society, without contests or anxiety of any kind, will be in the undisturbed possession of more advantages from wealth, and of more happiness, multiplied many hundred-fold, than have ever been enjoyed by the greatest possessors of private property, at any time, in any part of the world.

Under a rationally arranged system of public property, each one will feel himself to be sovereign of the world, with all its immeasurably increased advantages, which would speedily arise from the proposed change of system, and which increased advantages would be ever open to his use and enjoyment.

Possessors of what are called the largest amounts of private property, are continually subject to annoyances of various kinds, in their endeavours to protect it from being encroached upon by thieves, robbers, lawyers, or governments, local or general, and can never be without fears of private or public diminution of it; they must always, too, be on the alert to see that their own dependents are not cheating them.

Besides, it is usually found in practice that care and misery of one kind or another increase as private property, beyond a certain amount, increases.

But the arrangements of society, under a wisely constituted system of public property, will be so totally different, and so far superior to the present state of society under private property, that the inferior condition of mind and feeling produced by this last-mentioned system cannot in any degree realise the extent of the innumerable superior advantages that would be attained and enjoyed by the change.

Neither can good conditions be created under any human code of laws ever yet invented and brought into practice. What a mass of absurd contradictions are the English and American laws at this day—the laws of the two most advanced and powerful nations of the earth!

They are laws admirably calculated to create and perpetuate crime and misery. And who comprehends them? No man living, or who ever lived.—The greatest lawyer past or present was or is the most conscious of their obstruction to the formation of a rational state of human existence. They always have been made to oppose nature's laws—those laws which can alone make man to become good, wise, and happy, and which alone can unite him to his fellows in a cordial and permanent bond of brotherhood.

For men to think of forming universal brotherhood with existing laws, religions, Governments, law-made unnatural marriages, private property, and commerce based on the principle of buying cheap and selling dear, is a notion too absurd to be entertained by those who have attained only the first degree of common sense with regard to the right construction of society.

These defects in the formation of society have arisen from the past undeveloped state of the human faculties and powers; but the increased development of the present century has given to humanity new perceptions, to perceive truth from falsehood, good from evil, and right from wrong, so that these old defects are becoming too glaring to the multitude to be continued much longer. And such is the increased development of the human powers, that men will not now be satisfied with the little petty reforms of little petty reformists. The endless reforms proposed by the religious, political, and commercial reformers, amount to no more than means to arouse the attention of society to the immediate necessity for a reform that shall go to the root of all these evils, that shall reform man himself from his birth—physically, intellectually, morally, and practically—and shall thus enable him to effect at once the radical reform now so much required and desired by all sound thinking people in all countries.

The "wise" men of the world have taught, that to change from falsehood to truth, from wrong to right, from evil to good, from universally repulsive to universally attractive feelings, must be the slow work of ages, and must be effected step by step through many successive eras of generations, and wars of desolation and destruction.

This is an error, arising from imperfect development of our mental faculties. To change from falsehood to truth, from wrong to right, from evil to good, and from repulsive to attractive feelings, is but one step; and whenever it shall be made, it will be accomplished at once, as with every other new discovery and invention when fully made known.—There was no step between conveying intelligence by steam and by electricity, nor between the old mode of travelling on common roads and the new mode by railways. Neither is there any step between falsehood and truth, wrong and right, evil and good, repulsive and attractive feelings; and when this step shall be made from falsehood to truth, the step from wrong to right, from evil to good, and from repulsive to attractive feelings, will also be made. Truth will effect this great change, and truth alone can accomplish it; and yet there is no step or half step between falsehood and truth.

The world must continue to maintain this wretched system of falsehood and of counteraction to happiness, or it must openly decide, by the authorities of society, to abandon this system, and to adopt that of truth, and the direct and certain road to permanent and universal happiness.

Look at the present state of Europe, and the general condition of the population of the world, and say if it is possible that a sound thinking mind can see the slightest indications, in the government of any one nation, of common sense in directing the powers and capacities of its population to attain goodness, wisdom, and happiness.

And yet, see how plain and open is the road, and how easily and pleasantly it may be pursued, without meeting any obstacle to progress, much less any cause to stay by the way, or to retrograde, if truth were at once made the foundation of society.

"Yes," it will be said, "this may be all true, if truth were discovered; but what is truth, and how shall mankind distinguish it from error?"

Once for all, there is a mode to be adopted, by which, through the use of reason, directed by the experience of the past, truth, on all subjects the most important for man to know, may easily be distinguished from error or falsehood. The criterion is perfect. Truth is always consistent with itself, and is in accordance with all fixed facts and ascertained laws of nature.

". What, then,"—it will now be asked—" is the undoubted fundamental truth on which human affairs should be governed, and the characters of all men should be formed, to secure the well-being of each separately and of the human race unitedly through all succeeding generations?"

This is the question of questions, and on the true answer depends the future misery or happiness of mankind.

An attempt shall now be made to solve this problem, and thereby to give permanent progressive prosperity and happiness to humanity of every color and in every clime, and, ultimately, peaceably to give the extent of human felicity to every one from birth, so far as their created organization will admit.

There can be no difference of opinion among those who are permitted to think for themselves, and who have been taught to observe facts with attention, and to reason accurately from those facts, that man is created without his knowledge, with all his organs, faculties, and powers, physical and mental; and that he is unconscious by what mysterious power this most wonderful, spiritual, chemical, and mechanical machine has been formed and combined, and is kept during life in vital action and in perpetual working condition.

This mysterious creating and preserving power requires a name; and the nations of the earth agree to call that incomprehensible existence God. As, then, it must be admitted, as being a self-evident truth, always consistent with itself, and in accordance with all the known laws of nature, or of that mysterious power called God, that man knows not how to form any one of his natural qualities of body or mind, he can have no rational claim to merit, neither can he righteously be in any manner blamed or artificially punished for them. All punishment of man by man is artificial, and is opposed to the laws of nature; for God righteously, and always correctly for the good of the individual, punishes or rewards every action of man.

But man is born, or comes at birth into this outward world, with these mysterious spiritual, physical, and mental powers, in combinations; while each personal combination of them differs from all other individual combinations. Yet all these combinations are composed, although in different proportions, of the same general qualities; otherwise man would not be man, but would be some other kind of being.

It is a law of nature, or of God, that there are certain general external conditions which are unfavourable to the growth and full development of these wondrous powers of humanity — physical, intellectual, moral, spiritual, and practical,—while other general conditions are highly favorable to the growth and development of all these faculties, powers, and propensities,

Experience proves that it is a Law of God that man should be born helpless, and ignorant of good or bad, inferior or superior conditions; and that the rising or young generation has to depend upon the preceding adult generation for the inferior or superior conditions in which it shall be placed for its well-being, well-doing, and happiness, or for its ill-being, ill-doing, and misery. And that the existing adult generation has illimitable power, i it knew how to use it, to create, with the means now at its disposal, evil or good conditions—physical, intellectual, moral, spiritual, and practical—through the life of every child that shall be born. The means to effect this work are, by union of mind and action among all the sects, divisions, and nations upon earth.

It will now be said, that this union is impracticable; because it has never existed. Previously it has been stated, that by one step, and it is now reiterated, that by one step, taken in accordance with the now ascertained laws of God, truth shall be made to supersede falsehood, right shall be made to supersede wrong, good shall be made to supersede evil, attractive feelings to supersede repulsive feelings; and not in or for a sect, a party, or a country, but for all sects, parties, and countries, and for ever.

What, then, is this little grain of mustard-seed, or of truth, which shall thus govern the earth, and overwhelm or influence all of human-kind?

It is simply the knowledge that man does not

form himself, and that he is not responsible for the faculties forced upon him by the Creating Power of the Universe, or for the external conditions forced upon him by his predecessors in age and experience.

This is that germ of wisdom, which, in its progress through all lands and among all people, will burn up error and anger in man, and cover the earth with consistent and superior knowledge; and by which happiness for the human race will be established for ever.

Man will no longer be made the slave or servant of man; science will gradually become his most faithful and efficient slave and servant.

Already is science competent to be made speedily to supersede slavery and servitude of man to man. What is its present power? No man can estimate the extent it has already attained. It has the daily growth of a strong giant, with millions upon millions of arms, whose increase is illimitable, and who is more than competent for all human wants and purposes, when directed by the rare wisdom now to be derived from the most simple and certain of all truths—from a truth which will rapidly make all things upon the earth consistent, and man everywhere to become a rational being, ever good, wise, united with *all* his fellows, happy, and in daily delightful communion with his loved departed ones, and with holy angels, whose every desire is to progress humanity up to excellence and high rational enjoyment.

Who can estimate the power and value to-day of science in the British Islands alone?

When the writer was born, it did not probably much exceed, if it amounted to, a power equal to the labour of *twelve millions* of full grown men. It now far exceeds the labour of *one thousand millions*. Gas, steam, and electricity, have in this century added their but yet infant powers, under man's individual repulsive action, to swell this amount. But what is this puny attainment, compared with that which will arise when society shall be based on truth instead of falsehood, and when men shall be solely influenced by attractive, instead of by repulsive feelings, and shall become rational beings? Eighty years ago, science in the British Islands had but the power of about twelve millions of men to multiply its productive power annually. Now it has more than the power of one thousand millions of men to add annually to this already enormous amount. It may rapidly be doubled, trebled, quadrupled; for it is in its nature illimitable in its extent for the permanent benefit of the human race. If, then, less than the thirty millions of population in the British Isles have in less than a century made this progress in creating scientific knowledge and power, what have other populations been doing in the same period? And when all of our race shall be rationally placed, trained, and educated from birth, (which this glorious truth for the foundation of society will effect much more rapidly than mortals can now imagine,) what will *then* be the annual progress of scientific knowledge and valuable useable power? Where is the mortal intellect now equal to this arithmetic? Can mortal power, unaided by the assistance of spirits from the spirit world, enter into the calculations of this immensity of future delightful progress, and of its endless enjoyments?

But man is not sufficiently developed to believe these truths. His mental faculties have not yet been expanded to comprehend the good in prospect for himself and his offspring to the remotest period of the earth's being inhabited. The new, now becoming general, manifestations from the spirit world, are to become universal, and to overcome all mere mortal opposition, and are thus to progress the development of the human race, so as to compel all to believe in them, and to abandon all the prejudices necessarily emanating from a false training and education, and from the inferior and injurious conditions produced by a system based on falsehood, and with that falsehood permeating through all its ramifications over the earth.

The time is come for this change, and, as previously stated, for it to be commenced at once, by one step both in principle and practice. In principle, by adopting the truth, derived from all facts, that God and society create and form the character of all of human kind, and that society may now *well* form that character, by the practice of beginning to combine good and superior conditions only, upon new sites, leaving old society, false and injurious as it is through all its ramifications, gradually to die its natural death, in like manner as the old roads over the world are now dying their natural death where they are no longer useful, because they have been superseded by new roadways, so superior in principle and practice.

There has been for some time a contest between the principle and practice of complete independent individualism of man, and complete or universal association of interests and co-operation of action.

Both are erroneous; and both are impracticable under the existing system of falsehood and consequent irrationality.

The well being and permanent happiness of the human race require the union of these two principles, both complete, yet intimately combined in one harmonious whole over the whole extent of the earth :—perfect individuality, and perfect unity of co-operation, as far as both are compatible with the highest happiness of the individual and of society, and without opposition of feeling or of interest.

The wisdom of refined, good, and superior spirits, could alone suggest to mortals this new view of society—this high order of our future existence—this final redemption of the human race from ignorance, sin, and misery.

But who are to be the agents upon earth to commence and to carry forward this all-glorious work, for the redemption of mankind from the physical and mental bondage of evil? The existing authorities of the world, in Churches and States, are the destined mortal powers to commence, to direct, and to govern in peace and harmony, this change from falsehood to truth, from wrong to right, from evil to good, from repulsive to attractive feelings and cordial universal brotherhood of the human race.

Let those possessing the most comprehensive useful practical knowledge, make the practicability of this change, to be effected without disorder or confusion throughout all nations, plain to these authorities, and they will willingly adopt it, and will heartily aid in carrying it rapidly into execution, through all the divisions of the earth; and man shall be everywhere trained, educated, and placed, to become highly intelligent, consistent through life, or rational, and happy, with no one to make him afraid in the present or future; for pure love, which will then pervade all hearts and minds, will reign triumphant, and for ever will cast out all fear; and man will be wise and innocent as are now the superior spirits in the upper spheres of the spirit world.

Man is not made to resist his own happiness. But he is made to desire it through every period of his life. Therefore convince the authorities of the world in Church and State that there is another mode of human existence than the present, and one now easily attainable, a life altogether new to man, in which they, the present rulers of society, their children, and their children's children to the latest posterity, shall enjoy greater advantages and happiness, many hundred fold, than it is possible they can attain amidst any circumstances which men can devise under the existing false and irrational system. Ask the authorities of the most favoured nations to express the full extent of their present happiness and enjoyment, and when they reply in truth it must be that their life is artificial, far from peaceful, quiet, and real enjoyment, and, upon reflection, far from being at all satisfactory. Our Queen, Prince Albert, and their family, are probably surrounded by fewer annoying or fearful circumstances than any existing, or perhaps than any past ruling family, and yet, my knowledge of human nature, and of its feelings under the existing system of falsehood and error, compels me to know that a day cannot pass with them without physical or mental sufferings, regrets, or annoyances, which would not be experienced through the life of any one, born, trained, educated, and placed, as *all* would be, under the contemplated, true, new, consistent, and rational system of future society.

There is a daily and hourly strong inconsistency and glaring irrationality in the lives of all the present rulers of the earth. Ask President Pierce, the head of the most independent and progressive nation upon earth, what are his feelings now, as the legitimate and legal governor of the United States, compared with those which he experienced when in private life? His reply cannot be mistaken. He would willingly return to the latter, if public duty and the solicitations of interested friends did not retain him in his post of thorns. And so with the members of his Cabinet. Their conditions cannot be happy ones. Nor can those be of any statesman living. Even my old and highly valued friend Baron Alexander Von Humboldt, who has perhaps more heavenly or celestial feeling within himself than any other statesman living, must be often deeply and severely annoyed by the daily inconsistencies and irrationalities acting around him, and by vividly perceiving how much substantial and permanent happiness is perpetually sacrificed for the outward appearance of it, while the reality is poor and meagre, if not positive pain and misery. This artificial veil to the real misery of human existence, to the hollowness of a most unsatisfactory life, must now be withdrawn; all secrets will be made known; all hearts will be opened to the world; and no motive will exist to hide a thought or feeling from man to man, or from man to woman, or from woman to man; because nature forces all to have their feelings and convictions, and whatever God, through nature, forces upon humanity, is right and good, and, for the sake of truth, knowledge, and innocency, should be simply and honestly expressed. There is neither a bad thought nor a bad feeling in nature, or in man, except when nature in man is opposed and misdirected, as all men have been to this hour, through laws, customs, and institutions, arising from ignorance of their own nature.

*Truth, full* and *complete*, can alone make man and nations free.

It will be said by those knowing human nature imperfectly, that it will be impossible to convince the Authorities in Churches and States that it will be for their interests and happiness to change the system of falsehood and evil for the system of truth and good. Why should it be impossible to convince them of that which will be so highly and permanently beneficial to them, and to their immediate and future descendants?

Are they not human beings? Do they not desire their own happiness and the happiness of their children? Do they prefer evil to good, when they may easily abandon the one and secure the other? Can they make their own convictions in opposition to perpetually recurring facts? Have the would-be-reformers of the populations of the world ever applied with sufficient knowledge of the subject, and in a proper spirit, to these parties, and failed of their object? Never yet, since governments and churches have been established. No would-be-reformers have ever yet dived to the true foundation of error and evil, to effect a real reform in human affairs, or to explain a system that would truly place the Rulers of society in Churches and States *in a better position than those to which they have attained.* The principles and practices herein explained and recommended are *the first ever proposed to these authorities* that they could adopt with safety, benefit, and increased happiness to themselves and their children.

If Reformers propose measures that will be injurious to Rulers to adopt, it is unreasonable in such Reformers to expect that those possessing power should adopt them of their own accord. If the reforms proposed will be beneficial to the rulers,—let the reformers make this result plain to them, and their reforms will be adopted.

No parties can be satisfied under a system of universal falsehood and evil; but the Rulers of Society are not likely to abandon one system of falsehood and evil, for any other system based on the same errors,—and no other has yet been offered to them.

The most prominent persons who have departed this life within the last half century, who were deeply interested in the general improvement of society, without regard to class, creed, or country, were President Jefferson, Benjamin Franklin, Shelley, Dr. Channing, and, for two or three of the last years of his life, His Royal Highness the late Duke of Kent, and I may add, though less known, Grace Fletcher, the affianced of the late Professor Brown of Edinburgh, and whose loss to him and the world at the early age of nineteen cannot in any degree be appreciated, except by those who knew the goodness of her heart and the capacity of her mind. The spirits of these parties, all of whom, except Benjamin Franklin, knew me in life, and were full converts or favorable to the new views which I early in life advocated and published, have, in the kindest manner, and with extraordinary patience and perseverance, come to advise me as to further proceedings for the benefit of the human race, and to encourage me in the continuance of the measures which I have been impelled and deeply impressed to pursue from my youth upward. And none but those who have been favored by these manifestations can form any correct notion of the persevering patience, kindness, and unceasing aid, which they are willing and most desirous to give to those who are engaged in the work of endeavoring to do good to and benefit the human race, as one brotherhood and one family.

And it is most gratifying to observe how uniformly they discountenance all divisions of class, sect, colour, or country. Their object is to permanently benefit *all of humankind equally*, without reference to divisions of any kind. They uniformly say, "Do not dispute with those who do not and cannot yet believe in these, to them, new and strange spiritual manifestations; for," they add, "we will adopt means to convince all, without your doing more than stating the facts within your own knowledge and experience. The continual increase and reiteration of the facts which we shall make manifest to the population of the world, will gradually and peaceably convert all, and compel them to believe in this new mode of re-creating the character of man, and of re-constructing society over the world." And I have the most undoubting faith, from the facts which have been developed by these superior spirits, that their statements are true, and that all they communicate will come to pass. They say the human race is only now sufficiently developed to receive these spiritual truths and physical demonstrations.

I intended to reply to the article referring to these spiritual manifestations in the last number of the Quarterly Review; but the "dominant ideas" of the writer are so far wide of the subject, and evince such total ignorance of the confirmed and undoubted facts on which it rests, as upon an immoveable rock, that, in reply, it is only necessary to state those facts in a plain, simple manner, and the spirits will remove the notions of those obsolete, but yet, with some, "dominant ideas" from the public mind.

1st fact. The Media are the electric telegraph used by the spirits, and are unconscious how they become such.

2nd. The Media have no control over the spirits, but the spirits control them.

3rd. The Media know not whether any spirit will come when they ask for one; or, if one should

84        THE FUTURE OF THE HUMAN RACE.

come, whether it will come immediately or after much delay.

4th. When a spirit comes, the Media do not know what spirit it is, until, if to a rapping medium, it gives its own name by the alphabet.

5th. When the name is given, the Media have no knowledge what the spirit will say of its own accord, without any questions being asked,—or, if questions are asked, what the replies will be.

6th. The Media do not know how long any spirits will remain with them after the spirits have announced their presence.

7th. The spirits express themselves very much in accordance with their character when living upon the earth in the flesh.

These facts I have ascertained by close and accurate observation, beyond the slightest doubt in my mind. Whether others believe them or not is quite indifferent to me; because I am assured, by the most reliable spirits, that they will discover and adopt measures to force all to believe in them, and in their good intentions to attain the permanent goodness, wisdom, and happiness of the human race.

It is time now to come to decisive practical measures, and to what can be done for the human race, for its speedy development and permanent progressive advance and happiness; not for any particular division of people, but for all people through futurity and eternity. Partial measures, and the little reforms so far proposed by those trained and educated from birth in a system of falsehood, error, and repulsion, will not, if attained, make much change for the better in the population of the world for many centuries. Truth for the foundation, expansion of mind, and fearless moral courage to declare the truth openly, are now required to effect immediate substantial good for man, independently of all local prejudices, which must be overcome and destroyed.

Look now well at the population of the British metropolis, the most populous, wealthy, and learned in the world, and governed under one of the best of the governments by which the nations of the earth have been so long misgoverned. Inspect each inhabitant closely, from the extreme east to the west, and from the north to the south, and what do you discover? Much more than the Earl of Shaftesbury has discovered. Humanity, as created by the Great Creating Power of the Universe, called God, more or less in each one, but to a great extent in all, deformed and misdirected, physically, intellectually, morally, and practically.

Look, again, at each of the individuals inhabiting *all* the cities, towns, and villages over the world; and then at those living in *all* the country districts; and what do you see? equal deformity and misdirection.

"What," it will be now asked, "are there none,—not one, in the British dominions, or in the United States, — the present most powerful and pet nations of the world, who are not deformed, physically, intellectually, morally, and practically?" No, not one.

How has this arisen? Through the undeveloped state and want of knowledge of all the ruling and influencing authorities in Churches and States. They have not known human nature, or what the conditions are, or how to form them, in which truth, goodness, wisdom, unity, and happiness, could be created with the certainty of a law of nature. These conditions are now at the control of existing governments, which amply possess all the means, by the most pleasant unperceived force, to compel every one in future to become good, wise, and united, and by becoming good, wise, and united, to become also, whatever may be their complexion, beautiful and happy.

And more—as the Great Creating Power of the Universe creates only good faculties and qualities in the germ or spirit of every one of the human race, provided they are placed from birth in good natural conditions, or in conditions in accordance with their nature,—therefore, if any of human-kind in future should be deformed in mind or body, it will be owing to the ignorance of the governing authorities in Church and State. For these are truly the cause of all disunion, falsehood, and crime, and of every physical and mental deformity, among men. And if there were any rationality in human punishments, these parties alone should be punished for any crime committed by any individual under their control and government.

It is left for me now to say, that ignorantly-learned men will continue to endeavour to falsify and discredit these new spiritual manifestations; while by such proceedings they are doing as much injury as they can to all their fellow creatures.

Either the regular communication, as stated by myself and others, with superior spirits of our departed friends, is one of the greatest deceptions ever practised on human credulity, or it is the most important event that has yet occurred in the history of the human race. The impression made on my mind, and on the minds now of hundreds of thousands, is, that they are as really communications from the spirit world, as the reality that we now exist upon the earth. And the human testimony in favor of this conclusion is abundantly more than sufficient to establish any other previously unbelieved statement, however strong might be the opposing prejudices.

The British mind is eminently practical, and is unwilling to allow any matter, especially when of universal and deep interest, to remain long in suspense, if measures can be adopted to bring the subject to clear demonstration.

With this object in view I now emphatically declare, that it is an urgent duty of all Governments, but particularly of the British and United States Governments, to fairly, fully, and thoroughly investigate this now, or soon to be, all important subject, to its foundation, so as to leave not a shadow of doubt upon the public mind, after this investigation shall have been made and officially reported upon by both Governments, and thus to destroy the delusion, if it be such, or to confirm the most important truths yet made known to man for his future well-being and happiness.

Seeing and feeling its all importance to the speedy universal well-being and happiness of the human race, and to the downfall of the reign of falsehood, ignorance, repulsion, crime, and misery upon earth, if these prove to be true spiritual manifestations, I respectfully offer to the British Government, and through it to the United States and all other Governments who may be desirous of ascertaining the truth upon this contested question, the means and opportunity of testing the validity of the communications purporting to come direct from his Royal Highness the late Duke of Kent, President Jefferson, Benjamin Franklin, and other spirits of departed men and women, who, when in life, were known to be superior in their respective walks of life among their associates.

Let the Government appoint two well qualified persons, and I will appoint two, and let these four appoint a fifth, which number, with myself and the medium, will be as many as can conveniently and effectively at one time examine this subject. The parties will have every opportunity given them to detect collusion or error, if such there be, and also to ascertain the truth, honesty, and validity of the whole proceedings, if the facts shall prove them to be true, honest, and valid.

Those who know me will readily discover, that my sole object in making this proposal *is the immediate permanent good of the human race*, having now no other object to attain while I may be continued in this life.

I shall patiently await the deliberation and action of the British and other Governments on this proposal.

ROBERT OWEN.

London,
28th October, 1853.

## SPIRITUAL MANIFESTATIONS,

From October 12th, to November 7th, 1853,

*(Continued from No. 4, of the* RATIONAL REVIEW.)

On Wednesday, October the 12th, I had a seance with Eliza Finch, and the spirit of Grace Fletcher was present. She is a kind-hearted spirit, and I asked her to tell me what would be good for my cold. 'You must have some beef tea, and go to bed. Put a bottle of hot water to your feet. You should not go out in the damp. Do not forget to take beef tea at night when you go to bed, and wrap yourself up warm. Good bye—no more at present.'

After this the spirit of H.R.H. the Duke of Kent came. I asked His Royal Highness what he desired to say. He replied—'You must reason with ——, and ask him what makes the raps.—Good bye." I did reason with him before he left in the evening for London; but no impression in favour of the spiritual origin of these manifestations was produced in him.

Friday, 14th. Had a seance, with Eliza Finch for medium, at 11 a.m. Present, the spirit of the Duke of Kent. 'What does your Royal Highness wish to say?' 'You must ask questions.' The day before I had commenced to write a pamphlet, and I had now two sheets. I put them upon the table, and asked His Royal Highness whether he saw and knew the contents of them. 'Yes.' 'Is what I have written in them true and good, and should I proceed and make a pamphlet of them?' 'Yes.' 'And advocate the cause in the way I have commenced?' 'Yes.' 'And publish it as a separate pamphlet?' 'Yes.' 'Shall I send a copy of my new review to your daughter?' 'Yes.' 'And to Prince Albert?' 'Yes.' 'And a copy of the pamphlet when published?' 'Yes.' 'You said I had a mission to perform?' 'Yes.' 'Will you tell me what that mission is?' No reply. 'Shall I live long enough to accomplish this mission?' 'Yes.' 'Does your Royal Highness recollect that you wrote several letters to me?' 'Yes.' 'I gave several of them to be copied, and the originals have been mislaid: Can you inform me where I can find them?' 'No.' 'Shall I recover them again?' 'Yes.' 'Are they with Mrs. B.?' 'Yes.' 'Should I go to London to direct the distribution of the Review when finished?' 'Yes.' 'Should I return here again afterwards?' 'Yes.' 'Good bye.' 'Good bye.'

15th, Saturday. Eliza medium:—and just going to leave for London with Mrs. C——.

The spirit of H.R.H. the Duke of Kent announced itself by the alphabet. 'What does your Royal Highness wish to say this morning?' 'You must ask questions.' 'When Eliza goes from here, can I have any communication with you?' 'No.' 'When should I go to London?' 'In eight days.' 'When I go to London, shall I again meet your Royal Highness at Eliza's house?' 'Yes.' 'When I go to London, shall I be enabled to obtain your letters from Mrs. B.?' 'Yes.' 'Will Mr. and Mrs. C. become mediums?' 'Yes.' 'Soon?' 'Yes.' 'I will not trouble your Royal Highness with more questions this morning. Good bye.' 'Good bye,' responded.

Thursday, 20th October, 1853. Eliza Finch medium. Spirit present, the Duke of Kent. 'What does your Royal Highness desire to say this afternoon?' (It was between 2 and 3 p.m.) 'I Have often told you that you have an important mission to fulfil—I will explain what I mean by a mission. It is, that each one has either a long or a short mission. You have had a very important one to fulfil, and have got a still greater one to carry out. You have got to redeem the human race:—to show them their folly:—to show them their want of knowledge. Come to-morrow between two and three o'clock.' 'Does your Royal Highness see the papers of MS. which I now place on the table?' 'Yes.' 'Do you know their contents?' 'Yes.' 'Are they true?' 'Yes.' 'Are they good?' 'Yes.' 'Shall I publish them?' 'Yes.' 'Good bye.' 'Good bye.'

Friday, 21st October, 1853. Eliza Finch medium. Three o'clock was the hour appointed by the Duke of Kent, and the spirit of His Royal Highness was there to a minute. He did not object to the parties who had come in being present. They were Messrs. Featherstonehaugh, father and son, and Mr. Capern, Mesmerizer. I asked what His Royal Highness wished to say. 'I should like to speak to you about the human race. My friend, the human race has never been in a more progressive state than at present. All they now want is truth. The truth will make them believe us. Without they can get truth, they cannot progress. Many are too stubborn to be taught the truth. You must tell them not to go on groping in the dark. Soon they will see, and become conscious of their folly. You can ask questions.' I said, 'I have added more to my MS. Is what I have written in addition true and good?' 'Yes.' 'Should it be published?' 'Yes.' 'When will it be convenient for you to come here again to meet me?' 'Whenever you can conveniently come.' 'Will Sunday, at 10 a.m., be convenient?' 'Yes.'

Sunday, 23rd October. I was at Mr. Slater's a quarter before 10. Eliza medium. No spirit present. But at 10 o'clock to a minute the spirit of H.R.H. the Duke of Kent announced itself. 'What does your Royal Highness desire to say?' 'I will give you a reply to the Quarterly Review. You must tell the public, in the pamphlet which you are writing, that the result of the reasoning in the Review will not depend upon them, but upon truth and the testimony of the spirits. Tell them it is of no use to waste time in attempting to explain us. Had they truth on their side, they would not oppose good advice to them; but they would examine more, before they became convinced and opposed these spiritual manifestations. Tell them to pursue a different course, and to be charitable towards all mankind, and not to oppose these manifestations without having a knowledge of facts, lest they should be doing injury to themselves and to their fellow creatures, who would carry out their ideas. You must ask Mr. Slater why he does not like my saying that they should not follow their own ideas.' Mr. Slater had made some interruption about the word 'ideas' which he now explained was a mistake. While we were discussing this matter, the spirit of the Duke left us, and immediately other spirits announced themselves. I enquired by the alphabet what spirits were present. My two daughters (who always come first); my wife; my father; mother; brother Richard; President Jefferson; Benjamin Franklin; Grace Fletcher. I had with me the first thirteen sheets of my MS. for an intended pamphlet, and which I put unopened upon the table, and asked, 'Do you, my dear relations and friends, see and understand the contents of these MS. papers?' 'Yes.' 'Are they true and good?' 'Yes.' 'Should they be published?' 'Yes.' 'Will they do good by being published?' 'Yes.' I then asked if they had anything particular to say this morning. 'No.' I then asked of the spirit of my wife if our families in America were well. 'Yes.' 'In Germany?' 'No.' 'Is it our daughter who is ill?' 'Yes.' 'What is her complaint?' 'Tightness of the chest.' 'Will she recover soon?' 'Yes.' I then thanked them for their kind attentions in coming, and, being rather fatigued with close application to the previous proceedings, I bid them good bye; to which they kindly responded.

At Mr. Slater's, 26th October. Eliza Finch medium. Present, the spirit of His Royal Highness the Duke of Kent. 'What does your Royal Highness wish this morning?' 'You must ask questions.' 'Do you know what I have written for the pamphlet since I was last with you?' (Mr. Slater had asked me for the last sheet of it which I had written.) 'Is what I have written, (putting the other sheets of MS. on the table) 'true and good?' No reply. 'What is wrong or deficient?' 'You must get the other sheet from Mr. Slater.' I did so, and arranged the whole in regular order. 'Now I can tell you. They are true and good, and should be published.' 'Should I add much more to the pamphlet?' 'No.' 'Should I remain in London?' 'No.' 'Can you conveniently tell me what part of the country will be the best for me to go into?' 'Yes. The Royal Oak, Sevenoaks; and remain there for the winter. Sevenoaks is the best place you can go to.' 'Should I go soon to Sevenoaks?' 'Yes.' 'How soon?' In three weeks.' 'My friends Jefferson and Franklin told me that certain persons in America knew how to apply the principles which I advocate to practice. Did our friends mean that these gentlemen knew the details of the combinations of the new conditions necessary to be applied to practice to make all good, wise, and happy?' 'No; but they know the general outline.' 'Will these gentlemen be capable of rendering me much assistance?' 'Yes.' 'Will Horace Greely assist us?' 'Yes.' 'What will Andrew Jackson Davis do in these measures?'

## THE FUTURE OF THE HUMAN RACE. 47

'He will try to establish a community of his own devising.' 'Should I assist him?' 'Yes.' 'By going to him?' 'No.' 'By writing to him?' 'Yes.' 'Will Mr. Barker, who is now in America, and who went from this country, assist us?' 'Yes.' 'Are there any females in America who can give us assistance?' 'Yes.' 'Can you conveniently give me their names by the alphabet?' 'Yes. Mrs. Bell.' 'Of where?' 'New York. Mrs. Brown of Philadelphia.' 'Can you conveniently give me more?' 'Yes. Mrs Baldwin, of Philadelphia. Mrs. Brittan, of Boston. I will meet you again on Friday, at 3 p.m. Good bye.' 'Good bye,' I replied.

I may mention here that neither the medium, nor any one present, had ever heard the names which had previously been mentioned by President Jefferson and Benjamin Franklin, as stated in my Review, of persons willing to assist me in my work of universal reformation, or of those females who were now mentioned by His Royal Highness,—with the exception of Messrs. Partridge and Brittan, (whose first names were unknown to us)—Andrew Jackson Davis, and Horace Greeley. We do not now know whether the other names mentioned are the names of persons who have any real existence; but I have great confidence in the reliability of the spirits who gave me the information, and I await the confirmation of them from America.

I went to the medium at 3 o'clock on Friday the 28th, but a difference of opinion between her and her uncle prevented a seance; for no raps could be obtained. The spirits always strongly object to disputes of any kind. Their recommendation is always, forbearance, kindness, and love, andcharity to its utmost limits.

At Mr. Slater's, 29th October. Eliza Finch, medium. Spirit announced to be present, His Royal Highness the Duke of Kent. 'What do you desire to say?' I had brought much new and important MS. for the forthcoming pamphlet, and I placed it on the table, with the intention of asking His Royal Highness, after he had said what I expected he was going to say to me, what was his opinion of it. But he at once said, 'You must ask questions.' I then said, 'Do you know the whole of the contents of these papers?' 'Yes.' 'Do you approve of them?' 'Yes, yes, yes.' 'Should I publish the pamphlet as it now is?' 'Yes, yes, yes.' 'Shall I publish it soon?' 'Yes, yes, yes.' 'Will the Government accept the challenge for full investigation?' 'Yes, yes, yes.' 'Will you and our other usually attending friendly spirits assist me to convince the Government?' 'Yes, yes, yes.' On reflecting a morning or two ago, while in bed, upon the apparent difficulty which some of the spirits had to make raps loud enough for me, as I am somewhat deaf, to hear at all times distinctly, it occurred to me that the sound might perhaps be better heard through or from a hollow frame or box; and before commencing to-day, I asked for a band box, on which to try the experiment. The raps on this box were at once distinct, so that I could easily hear them. I now asked His Royal Highness if he could rap with more ease upon the band-box than upon the table? 'Yes'—emphatically. The Duke had previously told me that I should leave London in about three weeks, and go to Sevenoaks.—I said 'When I go to Sevenoaks shall I find any medium there or in the neighbourhood?' 'No.' 'Then I cannot have any communication with you there?' 'No.' 'Must I always come to London to have communication with you?' 'Yes.' 'Shall I publish the pamphlet before I go to Sevenoaks?' 'Yes.' 'Shall I apply for more publishers than I now have?' 'No.' 'Shall I write any more Pamphlets or Reviews after the present publications are out?' 'No.' 'What should I do?' 'Write your life at Sevenoaks. It will be the best place for you to do it quietly and systematically.' 'In what place at Sevenoaks?' 'The Royal Oak Hotel.' During this time the raps were continued in a beautiful manner, expressive of much pleasure and approval of what had passed, and the raps not ceasing while I was writing down my questions and his answers, I again asked if His Royal Highness wished now to say anything to me? 'No—ask more questions.' I said—'Some days since I stated to your Royal Highness that I was unable to reconcile man's free-will and the fore-knowledge of God.' 'Man has no free-will; and God knows the past, present, and to come.' 'Is this the time destined by God to redeem man from ignorance, sin, and misery?' 'By a universal law of progression, man is now arrived at the temple of great and mighty advancement. This answers your question.' 'Will all the other spirits who usually come to me with your Royal Highness confirm all that has been stated to-day by you.' 'Yes. Come to-morrow at half-past 10. Good bye.' After the spirit of the Duke had departed, I enquired if other spirits were present.' 'Yes.' 'Who?' 'President Jefferson; Benjamin Franklin; Shelley; and Grace Fletcher.' 'Will you inform me what you want to say?' 'Ask questions.' Putting my MSS. again on the table, I said—'Do you see and comprehend the contents of these papers?' 'Yes.' 'Do you approve of all which is written in them?' 'Yes.' 'Will they do much good?' 'Yes.' 'Do you approve of my going to Sevenoaks?' 'Yes.' 'When?' 'After you have published the pamphlet.' 'Should I write my life there?' 'Yes.' 'Can I have any communication with you there?' 'No.' 'Must I always come to London to have it?' 'Yes.' 'How often?' 'Once a month; and you should stay a week when you come.' 'Where should I remain during the week when I am in London?' 'At Cox's Hotel.' 'But they are in the spring often full with visiting customers?' 'They will be able to receive you.' 'Shall I add your testimony to the Duke of Kent's, at the end of the pamphlet?' 'Yes.' Addressing myself to the spirit of Grace Fletcher, I said—'Shall I send the Review and pamphlet to Mr. Fletcher?' 'Yes.' 'Was the Mr. Fletcher who called yesterday at the Hotel in my absence, and left his card, a relation of yours?' 'Yes.' 'What relation?' 'Nephew.' 'Should I call upon him?' 'Yes.' 'And give him a copy of my Review?' 'Yes.' 'Does your mother continue quite well?' 'Yes. 'Good bye.' 'Good bye.'

At Mr. Slater's, Sunday, 30th October, 1853. Eliza Finch, medium. Spirit announced by the alphabet, His Royal Highness the Duke of Kent.

(The prefix, 'His Royal Highness,' is always mine. His Royal Highness always announces himself simply 'Duke of Kent.') 'Will your Royal Highness state what you wish to say?' 'Each one has a mission naturally to perform.' Last night it occurred to me while writing down the previous *seances*, that I would add a dedication to the pamphlet, and I wrote a short one, which I gave to ——, to insert in it. I intended to ask the Duke if I should add the dedication which I had written to the other MS.—but, without a word being said this morning to any one about it, the Duke said, 'Get a dedication for the pamphlet.' I said, 'Will the dedication which I gave last night in MS. do?' 'Yes—Very well.' The spirit of the Duke then proceeded to say— 'Appearances will now yield to facts—but not so as to improve the world too much. You must try to come to speak to me to night at Mr. Hoyland's, but you must not be out late. Go there at six o'clock, and go home directly after I have spoken to you. I wish you to ask questions now.' 'Should I publish two editions of the pamphlet?' 'Yes—one very superior, the other a cheap edition.' 'Can my present printer, with his materials, print the superior edition, in the manner desired for the upper classes?' 'No—but he can print the second or cheaper edition.' 'Should I send the pamphlet to many members of both houses of Parliament?' 'Yes.' 'Will the pamphlet have a powerful influence over the Government and Parliament?' 'Yes.' 'Shall I add to the pamphlet all the *seances* which I have had with the spirits since those which are narrated in the Review?' 'Yes'—emphatically. 'Can you tell me if a Committee will be appointed to investigate this subject this year?' 'No—there will not be one.' 'Next year?' 'Yes.' 'When Parliament meets?' 'Yes.' 'Is it decided when Parliament will meet?' 'No.' 'Shall I consult Lord Brougham again before Parliament meets?' 'Yes.' 'Is your daughter the Queen a believer yet in the spiritual manifestations?' 'Yes, she is.' 'Is Prince Albert?' 'Yes.' 'Who is the most influential believer in these manifestations in the House of Lords?' 'Lord Brougham.' 'Can you give another?' 'The Duke of Cleveland.' 'The same in the House of Commons?' 'Yes—Peel.' 'What Peel?' 'Frederick.' 'Are there any scientific practical men believers, who have much influence in society?' 'Yes.' 'Who?' 'David Brewster; and Henry Butterworth, of the Glasgow Medical Institution.' 'Will Sir Joseph Paxton be useful to me?' 'Yes, yes, yes.' 'And Messrs. Henderson and Fox?' 'Yes, yes, yes.' 'Good bye.' 'Good bye. Good bye.'

At Mr. Hoyland's, Sunday night, same date. His Royal Highness the Duke of Kent. 'You must try to get your pamphlet out next Thursday week. You will find that it will have a good effect. I do not wish to keep you any longer.'

At Mr. Slater's, 1st November. Eliza Finch, medium. She had been ill, keeping her bed, from which she arose to come to give the *seance*; and before I went, Mr. C—— requested me to ask some questions for him.

The appointment to-day was with the spirit of His Royal Highness the Duke of Kent, and at three precisely, he announced his presence. I said, 'Would your Royal Highness wish first to say anything?' 'Yes. You must tell Mr. Slater to mesmerise Eliza. I will now address myself to you. You have a paper about which you desire to ask my opinion.' 'Yes, I have'—and I put a proof page of the superior edition of my intended pamphlet upon the table, and asked him if that specimen was as good as he desired for the best edition of it? 'Yes, it will do very well, and without any more ornament.' (I had intended to add some emblematic engravings, and this was to prevent my doing so)—'Do you know that I wrote to-day to Mr Van de Weyer, to ask for an interview with the King of the Belgians?' 'Yes—I know it'—' Did I do right in so doing?' 'Yes'—'Will His Majesty give me an interview?' 'Yes'—'Soon?'—'Time doubtful,— but next week or the week after.' 'I have sent a copy of my Review to His Royal Highness Prince Albert, for him and her Majesty to read—did I do right in this?' 'Yes'—'Will they approve of the contents?' 'Yes'—'Will the King of the Belgians remain in this country until my new pamphlet will be out?' 'No'—'Shall I send him a copy to Belgium?'—'Yes.'—'I sent a copy of my Review to Her Royal Highness the Duchess of Kent;—was this also right?' 'Yes.'

I then said—'Mr. C—— is very desirous of becoming a medium—will he become one?' 'Yes.' 'How soon? 'In a month.' 'Not in less time?' 'No.' 'Will Mrs. C— become a medium?' 'Yes.' 'In what time?' 'Uncertain.' 'Your Royal Highness in our last conference wished me to have the new pamphlet finished by Thursday week. Had your Royal Highness any particular reason for desiring it to be finished on that day?' 'It was because you will then finish your mission before you depart this life.' 'Shall I live to complete the writing of my life?' 'Yes.' 'Shall I live to see a community formed, composed of the conditions which I wish?' 'Yes.' Is it a proper question for me to ask how many years I have to live?' No reply. 'I shall be very glad to be with you, happy spirits, whenever the proper time comes.' Upon my saying this, the raps were many and long continued, and in such a manner as to indicate great pleasure and much rejoicing. I then said—'I should be most happy to be with you, but I do not wish to leave this life while I can do more good here to my fellow creatures than I can do for them in the spirit world.' This was also approved by the Duke. I then said (wishing to be correct), 'Does your Royal Highness see the questions and answers as I have now written them?' 'Yes.' 'Do you approve of them all as they are now written?' 'Yes, and meet me here to-morrow at 3 P.M.'

Wednesday, 2nd of November, at Mr. Slater's. Eliza Finch, medium (but suffering much pain in her side). Present, with her, Mrs. Slater and ——. At three o'clock precisely the spirit of the Duke of Kent announced himself. I said, 'Have you any objection to —— being present?' Some hesitation. (—— has been so far an entire unbeliever in these spiritual manifestations.) 'Will you allow —— to be present, although he is an unbeliever yet; but I wish very much to convert him?' 'Yes, he may remain.' 'As I desire to remove his doubts, and to convert him to become a true believer in these matters, will you assist me to convert him?' 'Yes' 'What will be the best mode to overcome his doubts? Will you now tell me by the alphabet?' 'Yes. When the time comes for him to be converted he will not try to disbelieve.' 'How long will it be before he will be made to believe?' 'One month.' 'What books should he read?' 'Spiritual Teachings.' 'Would you answer any question now direct to him?' 'Yes.' He was now put in direct communication with the spirit of His Royal Highness, and the following occurred. He asked, 'Does the spirit know the name of the deceased person of whom I am thinking?' 'Yes.' 'Will it tell me the name?' 'Yes. Susan Hopton.' This was not the name; and —— then asked, how it occurred that the spirit was mistaken. 'It is because I cannot see his mind clearly.' 'Why cannot the spirit see my mind clearly?' 'It is because I do not come into communication with your spirits?' 'Why, then, did the spirit say it knew the name thought of?' 'We do not say positively.'

I then renewed my conversation with His Royal Highness, and said—'You told me at our last conference that when I completed my new pamphlet my mission would be finished—in what way did you mean that it would be finished?' 'You would then become more prepared for new measures, when that part of your mission ended by the publication of the pamphlet.' 'I have a written question which I wish to ask your Royal

Highness.' 'Yes—I know it.' 'Is it all true?' 'Yes.' 'Shall I add it to the pamphlet?' 'Yes.' The question was thus put:—'I am strongly impressed with the conviction, in consequence of the facts which are quite familiar to me, that the means and knowledge, if they were now called into action by the governments of the world, instead of their armies of destruction, are abundantly sufficient to make our globe a paradise, surpassing the described garden of Eden, and its inhabitants, earthly angels. That this change can be effected simply by training, educating, employing, and placing all, as it will be for the interest and happiness of governors and governed that all should be trained, educated, employed, and placed. But that none can be properly trained, educated, and employed, until they shall be well-placed to attain these three results. Also, that neither of the three can be obtained separately.' I then asked His Royal Highness,—'Will the King of the Belgians give me an audience soon?' 'Yes.' 'This week?' 'No.' Has he yet decided?' 'No.' 'Will he give me an audience next week?' 'Yes.' 'Shall I have a letter from Mr. Van de Weyer on the subject?' 'Yes.' 'Shall I send a copy of the pamphlet, as soon as it shall be ready, to your brother, His Majesty the King of the Belgians?' 'Yes, yes.' 'And to His Royal Highness Prince

Albert for Her Majesty your daughter?' 'Yes, yes.' 'Should I go to Sevenoaks as soon as I have distributed the pamphlet?' 'Yes.' 'Should I publish the whole of this *seance* in the pamphlet?' 'Yes.' 'And what occurred between you and ——?' 'Yes.' 'After I go to Sevenoaks, should I make the writing of my life my chief business?' 'Yes.' 'Is the writing of my life part of my mission?' 'Yes. Come to meet me here on Friday at 2 o'clock. Good bye.' 'Good bye.'

All this time the medium was suffering great pain in her side, and as soon as the Duke had left me, she expressed a strong desire that the spirit of Miss Fletcher could be obtained to be consulted. In a few minutes this spirit announced itself to be present. I asked her if she wished first to say anything? 'No.' 'Will you tell Eliza, the medium, what will relieve her pain?' 'You must see that Mr. Slater mesmerises her very often; for she is suffering very much.' 'Should she take any medicine?' 'No.' 'Have you any more instructions to give respecting her?' 'Yes; she must keep herself very quiet, and sit up to be often mesmerised. Good bye.'

On the 2nd of November parties had applied to me in favour of a foreign lady, who was a clairvoyant, and who latterly had had the spiritual raps frequently, but who did not know how to make use of them, being ignorant of the mode of testing them by the alphabet, and being altogether inexperienced in these spiritual manifestations. I appointed to meet the parties at Mr. Slater's on Friday, the 4th of Nov., at 2 o'clock. They were there waiting when I arrived. The medium, as soon as we sat down, had raps; and when I enquired by the alphabet what spirit rapped, the response was, 'The Duke of Kent,' who promised to meet me there at this hour, and who, as usual, was punctual to a minute. I asked His Royal Highness whether he objected to any of the parties being present. 'No.' I then said, 'Will you speak first to me?' 'No—but you may now ask questions.' I said, 'Is Madame P— likely to become a medium?' 'Yes, and a powerful one.' 'What spirits will rap to her first?' 'Her mother, father, and family. They will rap now, and we wish her to try.' She did try: raps were made, and I was going to show her the manner of proceeding by the alphabet: but she was very timid, and was confused by what the spirit of the Duke had said. I was going to ask His Royal Highness some questions of my own, but he said, 'The new medium must have all the *seance* to herself, and you should not interfere with her proceedings' Her own spirits then requested her to play and sing: which she did, very beautifully. This, they said, was to calm her mind, and to produce harmony among the party. Thinking that she would be less timid if I were absent, and having other engagements, I left the party; but I learned afterwards that little more had been accomplished.

On Friday, the 4th of November, at the conclusion of my *seance* with his Royal Highness the Duke of Kent, I forgot to ask him to appoint a meeting; but on leaving, at the door, I arranged with Mr. Slater that I would be there on Sunday morning, 6th of November, at half-past ten, a.m.—at which time the spirit of the Duke, immediately on my asking what spirit was rapping, announced himself. I asked His Royal Highness if he would speak first. 'Yes—I was with you yesterday, when you were with the King of the Belgians' (I had said to the King that I regretted his time was now so limited, because I should have been happy to introduce the spirit of his brother-in-law, the late Duke of Kent, to him, knowing how much they had been attached to each other.) 'He will be,' continued His Royal Highness, 'very glad to be introduced to me, and I should also be very glad to be introduced to him as his spirit friend. He will hear me when he returns again to England.' 'Will he return soon?' 'In about three months. I do not wish to say more, but you may now ask questions.' 'Did I say yesterday to the King of the Belgians what you wished me to say?' 'Yes. 'And to Mr. Van de Weyer?' 'Yes.' 'Should I communicate with His Majesty the King of the Belgians through Mr. Van de Weyer, or directly with His Majesty?' 'Directly with His Majesty.' 'Will his Majesty have sufficient influence to unite the Sovereigns of Europe in peaceful measures?' 'Yes.' 'Will he be able to induce them to begin to change this old system of falsehood and evil, for the new, of truth and good?' 'Yes.' 'Will your daughter and Prince Albert assist to effect this change?' 'Yes.' 'Should I put a motto to the pamphlet?' 'Yes, yes, yes,' (with great animation.) I had written three different mottos before leaving home, to submit for the choice of his Royal Highness. They were numbered one, two, three, and read thus :—

No. 1—'The *first* coming of TRUTH, which was to the extent that the undeveloped state of humanity at that period could bear, was through Jesus Christ; and it was to inform the human race that, to attain goodness and happiness, they must love God and man. The second coming of Truth is to instruct mankind in the knowledge of the means *how* to love God and man, and that that time is near at hand, even now, in our day.'

No. 2—'The *first* coming of *Truth* was given through the agency of Jesus Christ, an inspired medium from his birth, who taught that universal charity and love could alone make men good and happy. This was as much as the then state of humanity would bear. The *second* coming of *Truth* is *now*, and it is to instruct mankind *how to have* universal charity and love; and thus, by making men happy, to show in practice their love for God.'

No. 3—'Truth alone can make man good, wise, and happy.

'The first coming of this Truth was through Jesus Christ, an inspired medium from his birth, to teach the world the necessity for it to acquire *universal love and Charity.*

'The second coming of Truth is *now*, to teach the world *how to acquire and practise* universal love and Charity, and thus, not in word, but in action, to prove their love to God.'

ROBERT OWEN.

I placed these mottos unopened on the table, and asked His Royal Highness if one of these would do. 'Yes.' 'Which of them? I will call their numbers. Should it be No. 1?' 'It is good.' Should it be No. 2?' 'It is better.'

Should it be No. 3?' 'Yes, yes, yes,' with evident great approval.

'Shall I add this *seance* to the pamphlet?' 'Yes.' 'Should I send the finished pamphlet to your brother-in-law?' 'Yes.' 'And to your daughter?' 'Yes.' 'And to Prince Albert?' 'Yes. Send it direct to my daughter, not through any one.'

His Royal Highness then said—'I wish our writings through Mr. Slater (who is a writing medium,) to be put in the pamphlet.' (Mr. Slater had some time since written by the spirits several pages of manuscript, apparently addressed to me, but unfinished.) I said, 'Will you enable him to finish it to-day?' 'No.' 'To-morrow?' 'Yes. Meet me on Tuesday next at three o'clock. Good-bye.' 'Good-bye.'

At the commencement of this *seance*, the medium (Eliza Finch,) had been so ill during the preceding day and this morning, that she had been confined to her bed, and she left it only when she heard my rap at the street door; and seeing her so ill, I was desirous to obtain the advice of our spirit physician, Grace Fletcher, the kind and ready prescriber for disease. I therefore requested the medium to continue the *seance*, and many varied raps were immediately made after His Royal Highness had departed. I inquired, what spirits were rapping; and, by the alphabet, the response was—My two daughters, wife, father, mother, brothers, son William, Grace Fletcher, President Jefferson, Benjamin Franklin, Dr. Channing, and Shelley. 'I am very happy to meet you all together, dear relatives and friends. Have you anything you wish to say first?' 'No, do you ask your questions.' I said 'Can you tell what will do Eliza Finch good under her present suffering?' 'Yes, quiet; and to be mesmerised by Mr. Kavanagh.' (On inquiry I found Mr. Kavanagh had occasionally mesmerised her.)

I then said, 'Did you know of my interview yesterday with the King of the Belgians?' 'Yes.' 'Did you all approve of what I said to His Majesty?' 'Yes.' 'And to Mr. Van de Weyer'? 'Yes.' 'Mr. Van de Weyer said he did not believe in these spiritual manifestations; but I told him he would soon be compelled to believe:— Did I say right?' 'Yes.'

'Are all my family in America well?' 'Yes.' 'And in Germany?' 'Yes.' 'Thank you, my dear relatives and friends, for thus coming to communicate with me, good-bye.' 'Good-bye,' repeated from each, by a different voice of rap,— each rap being unlike all the others.

On Monday, 7th of November, in the evening,

the medium, Eliza Finch, came unexpectedly to me at Cox's hotel, to visit Mr. C——, who being called away to attend to particular business, I enquired through the medium if any spirit was present, and immediately the spirit of His Royal Highness the late Duke of Kent announced his presence in his usual manner to me. I said—'Do you wish first to say anything to me?' 'Yes. You have often asked me how you were to instruct the human race. I will now explain a little more to you. You must never hold any arguments with sceptics who strive against the truth, who close their ears against all you tell them, and say that you are going to instruct them in what will lead them to a place of torment. You should simply tell them, if they think their way should be the right one, they should better explain themselves. You should tell them that you do not wish to turn them *from* their way to heaven; but to teach them the right way to it. If they will listen to you, they will not be sorry for all you have told them. But if they will not, they will be saying to themselves, "Oh! that I had believed more what he said!" Listen to me, and I will continue to direct you how to proceed. But now you must ask questions.' 'Has Mr. Slater finished the letter you mentioned yesterday morning?' 'No.' 'Will he finish it to-morrow?' 'Yes.' 'Should it be put in the pamphlet?' 'Yes.' 'Should I put this, and all the late *seances* in the pamphlet?' 'Yes.' 'Will it be convenient for you to meet me at the house of the media to-morrow at 3 p.m., as agreed upon yesterday morning?' 'Yes.' 'Was Grace Fletcher present yesterday when so many of my other friendly spirits rapped to me?' 'Yes.' 'Do you wish to say anything now?' 'No.' 'Then I will not trouble your Royal Highness any more to-night. Good bye.' 'Good bye,' with very many animated raps.

Mrs. C—— had afterwards, while I was absent, a very satisfactory *seance* with the spirit of her mother. When I returned, the party were at supper; and soon after, when the media were about to depart, the empty hat box, (on which I now obtain the raps so loud that I can easily hear them and can even distinguish the raps of one spirit from another,) was at hand, and I said, 'Just try if any spirit is now present with us.' The media placed their hands on the box, and immediately numerous different raps were made. On enquiry, this proved to be all the usual members of my family (eight), Grace Fletcher, T. Jefferson, B. Franklin, Dr. Channing, and P. B. Shelley. I asked if they had anything particular to say so late, (it was now near eleven o'clock.) 'No; but we come to bid you good night.' (They could only do so by the media being present.) I thanked them for their kind attentions, and bid them good night, which was responded to by each separately, with much apparent affection and kindness.

\* \* \* \* \* \*

The principles and practices herein advocated, are those which from my youth upward until now, without ceasing, I have endeavoured to place before the human race for its everlasting adoption.

ROBERT OWEN.

*London,*
*November 16th, 1853.*

# LETTERS

*Addressed by the Spirits of His Royal Highness the Duke of Kent and others,*

To ROBERT OWEN;

Through THOMAS SLATER, Writing Medium.

---

FIRST LETTER.

---

To ROBERT OWEN, Esq.

*4, Somers' Place West,*
*Sept. 10th, 1853, 11 o'clock, a.m.*

MY DEAR FRIEND,

I am at this moment irresistibly impelled and impressed to write something to you—not knowing the design or nature of what I am about to say—but your advanced mind and superior judgment in the administration of what is just and necessary for poor humanity, will (no doubt) pardon me, if what I may hereafter say should turn out only to be some Babel of my own, whereon I bestow time and words only for the world to talk about.

You, my friend, have passed through more than fourscore years, and have read many books; have written much; have seen a great deal of this world's vanities, its vice, crimes, offensive wars, induced and encouraged by ambitious minds. You have witnessed the march of science, and the application of the elements to perform what the bones and sinews of mankind never would nor could be able to accomplish. You have lived to see, that in the same ratio as wisdom and knowledge spread, does superstition die away. You have laboured hard to untrammel the mind of man—to divest him of weighty fetters that hitherto have bound him to a sphere inhabited by persons with minds unable, through ignorance, or prejudice, or the wrath of heaven, or blind infatuation, to appreciate the matter-of-fact principles which you have advocated and laid down for their benefit. Chaotic as your views may appear to some people, who say " pooh," and scoff at everything that does not fall within the scope of their limited imaginations, you have nevertheless done a good work, and are about to do a still greater and mightier work than you have yet attempted. Yes, my friend, the world may scoff—the ignorant may not for a little while understand you—sectarians may lift their feeble voices against you, and exclaim, ' Surely the man is mad '—and with epithets characteristic of such people, they may assail you while you circulate your experience, knowledge, and plans, until their minds become operated upon by the mission you will have fulfilled. You will have to tell them that the God of their faith and their senses must harmonise, instead of there being so much difference betwixt their faith and their senses. The apprehension of the presence of the *God of spirits*, by faith, goes down sweet with them; whereas the sensible apprehension of an angel or departed spirit dismays them. This must not long continue.

You will see, and will tell the world, that the spirits of our dear friends and relatives, though they do not at present vocally express it, do pity our human frailties, and secretly suggest comfort to us when we perceive it not.

You will tell them that the time has come for an immediate enquiry into the doctrines which the spirits teach, and for it to be tested whether they be of God or not. And if the value of mankind is known by works—*not* by *words*;—by *actions*, and not by men's corruptions;—so with the spirits, by their manifestations the world may know them.—T.

---

SECOND LETTER.

*Tuesday, 12th Sept.*, 1853, 12 *noon.*

MY DEAR FRIEND,

Another diurnal revolution of our planet has just been completed. The sun at the zenith, passing over the wires and webs of our optical instruments, and majestically culminating, *proceeds onward* steadily,—leaving us, on mother earth, to follow his example—to roll onward, and add another link to our chain of knowledge—another web to our vision of truth. And as, in the use of the transit instrument in the hands of the astronomer, the correct measurement of time depends to a great extent upon the accuracy and uniform division of his webs,—so does the usefulness of our lives depend upon the proper division and applications of the webs that constitute our minds. May we never be impeded in our transit through life by unequally placed or broken webs!

I said 'transit through life,'—I mean a transit into life, where minds exist superior to ours, who are at this moment impressing us with happy, wise, and holy thoughts, Natural and Divine—A Spirit life.

We have hitherto gone our own way in spiritual matters, for want of facts. But it was either our distrust, or our presumption, or our contempt, that carried us. But now, facts can be had in abundance, and good advice can be obtained from our spirit friends, whom God hath appointed to administer knowledge directly to us.

Yes, dear friend, Our spirit brethren tell us that they see our needs, and the necessity to stop the course of evil, which has hitherto kept civilised man so little in advance of savages. They see that nations and Governments, and human minds, have exhausted their stock of knowledge in making laws—in talking much—in devising schemes—in fact, in applying *unnatural* means to prevent the evils of society, *instead* of *natural* means (which may be had in abundance.) By punishing crime, instead of preventing it—by attempting to govern the WORLD by human laws, instead of by nature's laws, when not one amongst us can govern himself.

The spirits know that it is one of the worthy employments of good angels to make secret opposition to the evil designs which continue to prevail throughout the earth. They have already done much. Many a wicked act have they hindered, without the knowledge of the agent, that would have been. These guardians come now to uphold us, by removing occasions, or by casting in good instincts. As our few good endeavours have been hindered by prevailing evils, so now, shall our evil ones be hindered by good angels. These come not to us as false worshippers of their heavenly father,—making pompous shows, and fair flourishes of their piety,—but they come to reform mankind, teaching them to love one another with brotherly love—to carry out the beautiful and divine principles laid down by Christ, eighteen hundred years ago.— T.

---

THIRD LETTER.

*Thursday, 15th Sept.* 1853.

MY DEAR FRIEND,

I yesterday had some difficulty in preventing an intrusion on my time and business, that I might continue to address you, according to my increasing desire to carry out the design intended at the commencement, whatever that may ultimately turn out to be. The subject of this letter will be confined to the phenomena that are creating such sensation in America and Europe, known as Spirit Manifestations, Table Moving, &c., and admitted by some philosophic minds to be natural phenomena. By "natural phenomena" is meant any motions or situations of persons and things among one another, which offer themselves to the notice of our senses, and are not the *immediate* acts of an intelligent being. Our modern philosophers say, that so apparently wild and extravagant are the believers in these phenomena, that it is hard to determine whether they are more distant in their sentiments from *truth*, or from one another; or whether they have not *exceeded* the fancies of the most fabulous writers, even poets and mythologists. But this is owing to their neglecting or declining to investigate or EXPERIMENT. Experiments, strictly observed, are the most necessary helps to the finding out CAUSES, and proportioning them to their proper EFFECTS. Without *observavation*, it is impossible we should discover the phenomena of nature—without *experiments*, we must be ignorant of the mutual actions of bodies, and uncertain whether the causes assigned be adequate to the effects which we would explain.

Our knowledge concerning external objects is grounded entirely on the information received through the medium of the senses. The science of physics considers bodies as they actually exist, invested at once with all their various and peculiar qualities. Its researches are, hence, directed by that refined species of observation, which is termed *experiment*. And it is the nature of genuine science to advance in continual progression. Each step carries it still higher. New relations are descried; and the most distant objects seem gradually to approximate.

But while science thus enlarges its bounds, it likewise tends uniformly to simplicity and concentration. The discoveries of one age are perhaps in the next melted down into the mass of elementary truths. What are deemed at first merely objects of enlightened curiosity, become in due time subservient to the most important interests.

Let, then, all examine, and we will tell them how; and their spirit friends will rap upon their *understanding* and upon their tables, and they all soon may perceive the spirits stand erect in conscious integrity, and dispensing blessings of every kind around them—not *as idle lookers-on* upon the wickedness of the times. For as this earth is made for action, and not for fruition, they tell us it is not enough FOR US to stand gazing upon this wickedness, although with tears, unless we endeavour to redress it. But not with *ceremonies*. Ceremonies must give place to substance. God will have mercy, and not sacrifice.

False devotees may scandalize, and may pronounce their verdict in favour of the *Devil!* Poor souls! they must be pitied, so long as they see *Satan* in everything. They see him in everything, because they fulfil the law without any *labours* of the mind—without any effort of the imagination! Scruples in spiritual matters torment their minds. But let them be told that nothing retards the soul so much in the way of truth and piety *as ill understood scruples*. To understand these things, they must examine them again and again, determined to cast their fabled Satan under their feet; and instead of putting questions to their spirit brethren, which are calculated only to satisfy their weak sectarian prejudices—let them ask for *heavenly* truths, and soon will they behold that their once esteemed and much-respected friends are not transformed into spirits of wickedness and servants of the old serpent, but are truly labouring to establish *Christianity*—UNTARNISHED—without spot—without a dissentient voice—without apostacy. Can bishops and their clergy—clergy and laity—in fact, all the diversity of sects that people the earth—say that some important, alterations are not needed to establish one great, grand and holy principle of unmistakeable truth:—a truth which all may see, and by seeing it, may understand the laws of God alike? Echo answers—"Yes! important alterations are indeed needed!"—And in waving undulations spreading over the vast extent of the earth, it asks derisively or despondingly, "Who shall—who will—or *what* can, perform and carry out this mighty feat?"

Can Reason only do this much longed-for work? Nay, it cannot:—because it is prone to listen to the passions and the senses, and is liable to build for itself frightful precipices.

Can our colleges and academies? No—surely. All the academics in the universe may imagine systems respecting the creation and governing of the world; but after all they have done or can do—after all their researches, conjectures, and combinations—after multitudes of volumes written on the subject, they will tell you less—*much less*—respecting it, than CHRIST has said in a single page. And as they continue to teach things which have no probability, it is evident that they, as they are at present constituted, cannot bring about this important change.—T.

## PRESERVATION SERVICE

SHELFMARK 10006 DF25

THIS BOOK HAS BEEN
MICROFILMED ( 199 7 )
N.S.T.C.
MICROFILM NO *SEE RPM*

Lightning Source UK Ltd.
Milton Keynes UK
UKHW052302130921
390416UK00010B/287